Love in Liquid Modernity: Rethinking Relationships

Varsha Bhargava

Published by Varsha Bhargava, 2024.

While every precaution has been taken in the preparation of this book, the publisher assumes no responsibility for errors or omissions, or for damages resulting from the use of the information contained herein.

LOVE IN LIQUID MODERNITY: RETHINKING RELATIONSHIPS

First edition. February 6, 2024.

ISBN: 979-8224729814

Written by Varsha Bhargava.

Introduction

Nothing is more characteristically human than the need to relate to others.

Someone could contest this statement by saying that irrational beings also need to relate to each other to fulfill their most basic needs, that communal life is at the foundation of the survival impulse itself, and therefore, we could be certain that our craving for relationships is primarily a trait of our animal side.

But there's something deeper in the human impulse towards others.

The reason is simple: humans are capable of love. In fact, more than capable, humans *need* another to love, for it is through surrendering to the other that the detachment necessary for love's manifestation occurs — as the poet once said: *What can a creature do but love among creatures?*

To relate to someone is to surrender to someone. This is the silent motto that separates those who love from those who use. Sacrifice for the other, the desire to make the other a better person, to bleed for the other — which, in extreme cases of love, has a meaning much simpler than that of a metaphor. All of this might sound like a very heroic and "romantic" discourse, but a sincere examination of our direct experience with love, both when we are loved and when we love, or when we witness the love of others, will only confirm it.

I'm not advocating here that we assume a lofty ideal just to sustain a grandiloquent discourse, but in total disagreement with life, because what I'm seeking is a fair and real view of relationships. This is what I want you, reader, to understand through this book: relating is an art, and like every art, it has its techniques, its exercises, its principles. Those who practice it need to be patient and humble, like every apprentice. They need to slowly change themselves to better perform it, ordering their interior so that their better understanding reflects in their actions. It is for this art that I intend to make my contribution.

To relate to others is not an option, and, more especially, only a few can abstain from carnal relations — here I speak of those who have a consecrated life. Aristotle already perceived this, when he said more than two thousand years ago that the solitary man is either a beast or a god. But even those who choose greater solitude are not completely exempt from relationships, but from a part of them. They navigate this world aloof from carnal relationship, but also live to love others on other, more subtle and profound levels. In short, no one can say to themselves, "this matter is not for me." Romantic relationships impact everyone.

And to say that they impact everyone is the same as saying they are a problem for everyone. There is no person who does not experience disruptions in their relationships, even the most balanced, even the kindest, even those we could call saints — all of them have experienced difficulties in their relationship with other human beings.

We are in the world to love our neighbor. Therefore, this is a central issue for human beings. It is necessary, however, to better understand what love means. I will not dwell on philosophical explanations and detailed discussion of concepts; it is not our purpose here. I will simply synthesize the theme, which is of the highest depth, into a practical and immediate concept that must be absorbed as a starting point for our healthy relationship with others:

The only love worthy of that name is selfless love.

Selfless Love

Let's start with a practical example: a marriage. From there, we can easily draw analogies to other forms of relationships. I acknowledge that it may seem strange to address the elemental foundations of relationships by directly discussing the most complex human relationship there is, but this is the fundamental point that needs to be understood, the goal that will guide all practical means to improve our ability to relate.

Selfless love is the central virtue for a marriage, for selfless love is that which is completely focused on the needs of the other. It is a love in which no selfishness, no personal interest enters; it is a gratuitous surrender.

It seems that this love is a love without intensity, since it will be selfless — and this is where many make poor judgments of solid and loving marriages by not seeing "passion" in the couple. This is because this lack of interest is not about the other, but

a lack of interest in oneself.

If in a marriage, on many occasions, we do not set aside our interests in favor of the spouse, the relationship becomes impossible. It becomes a war of interests, a permanent political and diplomatic tension, a trade of emotional exchanges full of selfishness. A permanent state preliminary to a war.

Selfless love is the opposite of this, and it is the antidote to it. It is a love without expectations, which does not expect the other to reciprocate as if with every loving gesture, with every good deed of yours, a debt were incurred that needed to be repaid at some point. The only hope that selfless love allows itself to have is that its influence generates positive effects on the loved one. And yet, this hope cannot be the foundation of this same love, but its consolation. Because it must exist from a root so generous as to not demand any kind of reward. Those who love selflessly soon understand that the fruits of their love are not visible, although they are very real, because this love produces a secret alchemy in the heart of the other.

Here, to progress, we will have to understand something about the Theory of Personality Layers, developed by Professor Olavo de Carvalho, which sheds light on some psychological movements present in this dynamic. Olavo understood that

**human personality is the expression of various
degrees of self-awareness**

which manifest through dominant objects of interest, which, in turn, adjust the movements of the entire personality.

Each dominant object of interest corresponds to a layer of personality, and the progressive journey of the personality through the interests, longings, and motivations of each layer ideally corresponds to full human development, on a chronological scale.

These are the twelve layers of personality and their correspondences in human development:

1st layer Body consciousness

2nd layer Physical or psychophysical constitution inherited

3rd layer Cognition and articulation between perception and action in the world

4th layer Emotional affirmation

5th layer Personal affirmation, of individuality

6th layer Affirmation in vocation and aptitudes

7th layer Affirmation in social roles

8th layer Personal maturity, assessment of one's own life

9th layer Intellectual personality

10th layer Transcendental self

11th layer Self-affirmation on the historical scale

12th layer Man before God

In the third layer, experienced in early childhood, reason begins to become aware of the external world. It is the time when children handle many objects with curiosity, fit pieces into corresponding spaces in a box, and are fascinated by the most insignificant trinkets. The process of this stage consists of a gradual apprehension of the physical world, and those who live in the third layer undergo a process in which their reason calculates to find stability from this same external world.

The transition between the third and fourth layers is lengthy because a sufficient accumulation of sensory experiences and historical living is needed for that personality to feed the bases of its emotional life. In the maturation stage represented by the fourth layer, reason continues to make calculations, but instead of operating on the external physical world, it turns inward, eager to explore its inner affections and emotional dimension.

The exploration of an inner world begins, of an affective territory that also needs to be traversed for the individual to feel stable in the world.

People in the fourth layer are constantly making emotional calculations.

They have not yet traversed this world enough to feel stable. Those who live in the fourth layer are like a child contemplating the way their toys fall, investigating how falls happen in various ways. But instead of toys, the individual living in the fourth layer investigates the effects of the world's influence on their affective and emotional life, in order to seek stability and acceptance. It is the person who worries about an approving glance, about a gesture that may seem rude, about a probable mockery.

This individual needs to constantly process others' affection internally to ensure they are being loved and accepted in this world. The sensation of someone in the fourth layer is that of never feeling sufficiently loved, a consequence of their excessive need to understand the affective dynamics around them. This person always grapples with a difficult question, to which they have no secure answer: "Do people like me?".

Everything becomes self-referential. In a relationship with a boss, for example, in a work environment, every interaction will not be understood in its objective sense, in the form of orders, projects, observations, etc., but taken as an affective relationship.

Therefore, any natural situation of demand or criticism is not understood in its objectivity, but as confirmation of personal disdain from the boss towards the employee, who might say: "The boss was harsh with me, does he not like me?". Meanwhile, from the boss's objective point of view, there was no personal dimension in the criticism, only an objective evaluation in pursuit of results.

This same example can be replicated in various relationship contexts. For the person in the fourth layer, everything is an affective relationship, making them an emotional individual. Being emotional in this case does not mean abandoning the use of reason, but a stage of maturity in which the operation of reason is very much concentrated on their emotional self-affirmation.

Romantic relationships between individuals in the fourth layer will be profoundly selfish, as there is an intense need to feel wanted and loved. A person living in this layer will tend to feel constantly frustrated by not receiving the due reward for their loving actions, in a strange and petty

emotional accounting.

There is a constant need to feel loved.

From there arise relationship problems, such as emotional blackmail, as relationships can be reduced to a mere emotional trade from which the individual cannot exit without profit. This is a serious obstacle to the exercise of selfless love, which is to some extent inaccessible to those dominated by the emotional self-affirmation needs of the fourth layer. It is a virtue of a more mature human being, who has been able to rise above this more fundamental dimension of the need to receive affection.

However, going through the fourth layer is part of the natural process of human maturation. It is not possible to skip this stage, and we all need to overcome it in a healthy way. Generally, children who had loving parents or caregivers in early childhood, and experienced the effects of truly selfless love within themselves, tend not to develop vicious habits related to the fourth layer.

To begin with: two practical exercises

As we have seen, the practice of selfless love is the goal of romantic relationships. It is the target we must pursue to be better partners to those we intend to love and to be people capable of conveying greater value in our relationships. Despite the great difficulties seemingly linked to this practice, the realization of selfless love will not be impossible, even for an adult still in the stage of the fourth layer. But to develop superior capabilities, dedication to its conscious practice is necessary, according to our strengths. It is not necessary to start everything perfectly. No skill is acquired overnight in its ideal form, but constant practice, care in always acting according to the goal, even in the details, builds its mastery day by day.

Now that we have outlined the goal of romantic relationships, I want to propose to the reader, as a starting point, two exercises to begin our journey in pursuit of selfless love. If you commit to them, no matter how strange they may seem, I guarantee you will notice a positive change in a short time.

The first of them is the practice of a *forced smile*. Simple as that. It is not always appropriate to express our feelings without any control. A great exercise in emotional control and dedication to others is the forced smile. First, because it is not pleasant, but it can hold an intention to produce good for the other, to create an atmosphere of well-being so that the other understands that we are at their service.

Many times, we needlessly unload our fleeting emotional states onto others, and in the face of some annoyance or discomfort, we transmit our bad feelings, creating a sour and unpleasant atmosphere. Being a source of relief to others, of greater lightness, even consciously forced, is also being a source of joy. This reverberates even in the biochemical and osmotic dimension of human relationships.

> **We don't need to absorb the energies of the environment, but to give others energies that uplift their spirits.**

It's the alchemy of contamination by goodness. Emotional intelligence is the ability not to be contaminated by others' feelings and not to let others be contaminated by your bad feelings. It is consciously acting to transmit emotional strength in a troubled environment. To contaminate others with positive feelings.

It may seem silly; after all, what is a forced smile? But this practice is a form of charity, and charity is the only virtue that remains even after death. We won't need faith anymore (everything will be revealed) or hope (everything will have happened), but charity, love, will remain. Now, we who are weak, what reason would we have to despise even a particle of possible charity? Persist in this practice over time. The effects will happen, and the people around you will be changed. Smile without will, until the smile

becomes natural. It is very simple to smile. It requires little energy. The smile is the smallest particle of our charity towards others. Do not underestimate the power of a smile; few people can deal with difficult relationship problems, but anyone can smile. The smile breaks something in the other person, and its power is magnificent; it is a simple act with wonderful effects. Smile without thinking, smile to everyone, and especially to those who want to give themselves.

The second exercise was also passed on to me by Professor Olavo de Carvalho, who taught it to his students in his philosophy courses. Imagine that the lives of others are a novel. Think of the other person as the main character of a story, their story, which is a story full of important characters, decisive events, dreams, loves, aspirations, just like yours.

Thinking of each life as a life with its own narrative and depth destroys in us the contempt we might feel for others. Generally, in our selfishness, we see others' lives as mere outlines. "So-and-so is a doctor, graduated from somewhere, today is the director of a hospital and earns a lot of money to travel every year." This is the summary and cruel look we easily use towards others.

When we think of other lives as the true stories they are, it takes us out of a worldview centered on ourselves. Thus, we no longer see people as mere functions in our story, as extras in our life, but as men and women full of our same life.

There is no uninteresting life. There are lives that do not interest us.

With this exercise, your life ceases to be the center of the universe, and you will even allow yourself to admire someone who would never have your interest; to consider another person truly remarkable, not out of envy, but by glimpsing the great dramatic force of a life in action. Thus, when you least expect it, selfless love will begin to flow and take root in your heart. You will see that

Human beings have profound value, and there is no greater honor than serving a loved one,

a being of this incredible species crowned with glory. Here is the beginning of your selfless love, a love that wants nothing in return, but will always be "in the empty shell of love in timid search, / patient, for more and more love."

Be Interesting

———

Many might think that in this chapter I will discuss tricks to make someone interesting. But that's not it. No one can become interesting overnight. There's no ready-made formula for it, nor techniques to automatically make someone interesting, and I believe anyone who promises that is lying. Because it's not enough to *seem* interesting, one must be interesting. And the difference between being and seeming is quite significant, requiring a deeper and more sincere effort than magic tips can provide.

First of all, when it comes to the role of interest in a romantic relationship, it's necessary to acknowledge that the initial impact of appearance is an important factor. Experience proves it. When we enter a new environment, we immediately find people interesting, even without knowing them. It's clear that there's an aspect that generates attraction on its own, which is appearance. Often some experience the phenomenon of "love at first sight" because of this. This attraction is improperly called love because this type of affection, being instantaneous and based entirely on superficial aspects such as appearance, subtleties of personal posture, the way someone moves, or how they talk, etc.

But the intention here is not to dismiss these external personal characteristics.

We should never underestimate the aspect of appearance.

We need to maintain ourselves presentable, attractive, well-groomed, and moderately vain. These concerns should not be eliminated, so take care of yourself. This is a care that especially applies to singles still seeking a relationship and who depend more on the first impressions generated on potential partners.

Immediate impressions do not reach the person's interior, their being. It's very rare for interest to arise, as it often appears in novelistic situations, based entirely on a person's "inner" self. We need to be realistic and admit that we are only interested in the interior of those who first attracted us externally. It's natural that an appearance or presence with unpleasant or repulsive traits never inclines us to deeper contact. Even among partners of years, where daily coexistence naturally allows for a certain neglect in appearance, remaining pleasant and attractive as much as possible is important for maintaining the relationship.

Maintaining oneself as a physically pleasant and well-groomed presence has an immense impact on the pursuit of relationships. At first, the other person doesn't know what's inside you. The initial attention grabber, which can develop into a lasting relationship with deeper consequences, is the pleasant appearance. This is an undeniable, even obvious fact, but it's worth repeating.

However, my interest in this book, in dealing with human relationships, is to go beyond, to provide you with the means to build a lasting relationship that sustains itself in a deeper interaction. There's no archetype older and more known than that of the person who combines extreme beauty with total superficiality.

Beauty matters, but it's not enough.

Undoubtedly, beauty is a value, but truth is a greater one. It's a badge to promote you in first impressions, to place you as a potential object of immediate interest, but it will never replace human mastery, your inner mastery.

You need to commit not to appear, but to *be* an interesting person. And to be interesting, in this deeper sense, what matters is not what reaches others' eyes, but what comes out of your mouth and reaches their hearts. Because what "comes out of the mouth proceeds from the heart," and thus the criterion of truth in human relationships is always a heart-to-heart conversation.

Now, carefully think about the people you admire the most. Try to remember what is so absorbing about them that they have a special place in your heart. Does all this magnetism stem solely from their appearances? Or does it come from their values, their kind words, their wisdom, their character, their noble actions, their generosity, and optimism in the face of adversity? Notice how the factors that produce greater admiration belong to the realm of language, to the realm of expression. The most interesting people are those capable of communicating with greater depth and richness. It's not just about communicating well or eruditely (because many may simply confuse this with rhetoric or pseudo-intellectualism), but transmitting good words, transmitting wisdom.

And what did these people do to speak well and wisely? They nurtured their inner selves with an intellectual and personal repertoire that made them capable of drawing clear views and intelligent ideas from their life experiences. This is the result of study, of a sincere dedication to a better formation of the spirit. Not without reason, the expression "presence of mind" retains some of this ancient sense, this mysterious something extra that exists in interesting people. It's for this person that others grant their attention because she has something valuable to say. Whoever says something of value also has value. They are an interesting person.

You need to dedicate part of your time to this pursuit. It's necessary to employ your efforts to become an internally interesting person. We can keep in mind the saying that goes: "to be interesting, you need to be interested." That is, you need to be the opposite of a superficial person, to whom nothing matters, who is always unwilling to add something new to her baggage, always wrapped up in her own interests, with her small pleasures, relishing even with pleasure her own ignorance and pride, usually abandoned to the successive waves of trends and unable to say anything beyond what is said in the *show business*, or what is imposed by *pop* culture, or by the shallowest mediocre opinion of newspapers.

To attract people, you need to let yourself be attracted first by things, because only through this absorption of the things around you will you be able to fill your baggage with stories, ideas, knowledge, and intriguing perspectives. By doing so, you'll expand your repertoire of psychological awareness, being able to navigate through more topics, developing your sensitivity to see more situations with interest, and refining your aesthetic refinement by understanding, through the increasingly larger sampling of this imaginary baggage, the significant difference between what is shapeless and what is clear, beautiful, and meaningful.

The three pillars that make someone interesting

I consider there are three fundamental characteristics for someone to be interesting. Unlike magic tricks that won't make anyone interesting, but at best will produce an empty appearance of someone with this characteristic, these qualities I will talk about can only be achieved through continuous and long effort because such characteristics compose the nature of someone who seeks to be, that is, someone who makes an authentic effort to be present, real, and not a shadow of the sum of appetites and interests that superficially float in society.

The first pillar in building the capacity to be interesting is

attention.

You need to be attentive, have a total presence in the world. It's not uncommon for us to enter our social circles totally scattered, totally unaware of where we are, inattentive to everything. You will need to direct your attention to people and things to draw something from them. Your dedication will require attention as its greatest prerequisite because without attention, nothing presented to us can be absorbed.

It's the effort to abandon the "automatic mode" of living. It's to be effectively present in all your actions, with an active level of consciousness to absorb things from the world and draw from them contents that can fill your inner self.

The second pillar is

generosity.

Do the same exercise as at the beginning of the chapter: think now of the people who seemed interesting to you throughout your life, who captured your attention. It's not surprising to find that the vast majority of them—or even all of them—were not self-interested and selfish people, right? You didn't perceive in them any intention to steal something from you, to take a reward for themselves, as if they were in a business deal.

Let's note that the people who were (and are) interesting to us were precisely those who were capable of taking an interest in us. It's a fact proven by everyday experience that people who show more interest in others are the ones who also attract more interest from others.

The exact opposite of this interesting type is someone who, in any conversation or interaction, is only capable of making incessant references to themselves; who only has interest in talking about their own things, their impressions, their story. Honestly speaking, this type of person is a bore. This attitude doesn't hold anyone's attention. The self-referential companion is the proverbial "drag," the one who, with much luck, if surrounded by charitable people, receives complacent attention from listeners, who discreetly look at the clock, hoping the ordeal will end soon or if there's a reasonable excuse to escape the horrible conversation. For the "drag," the other is just another extra in their story—and in their story, there's no one important except themselves. They see the other as just a listener, not a companion.

Every very self-referential person will lose the attention of others. Therefore, generosity is an effective remedy against the danger of focusing too much on ourselves. It's through generosity that we can have a genuine interest in what others have to say, in what they feel, in what they are. Generous people are willing to serve and give without asking for anything in return. That's charming. To be generous is to be extremely interesting.

The third pillar is

consistency.

The charm associated with the previous two pillars loses much of its attracting power if your actions are practiced only sporadically. The true joint attracting force of these pillars is only realized when these acts are consistently practiced. When you're able to apply your sincere attention consistently and to have a charitable posture continuously and frequently, the potential to become an interesting person increases significantly.

Let's not allow these pillars to be merely the backdrop of a "bright night" in which we perform wonderfully well in some social situation. We can be very interesting for a day, but these episodic good performances don't mean we've become interesting. That's why these practices require consistency and frequency, a true change of perspective towards life and others. This new way of interaction, as it gains an increasingly positive and natural character, begins to effectively alter our inner selves, and then, after a while, we become interesting, not just seem to be.

Being interesting takes effort. No tip, no movie, no psychological archetype, no consultant, and not even this book will make you interesting. That's because being interesting requires a commitment to wanting to be so, a commitment that needs to touch intimate strings within ourselves and consistently change our posture.

The difference between being interesting and being manipulative

We must be careful not to confuse those who have a genuine interest in others, and therefore lend them attention and consistently act generously, with those who apparently give attention but do not generously give themselves to others—many end up being deceived by impostors, given the immense attention deficit our scattered world has created. Those who apparently pay attention harbor a hidden interest, a secret selfishness that desires to satisfy through an initial seduction, so similar to genuine attention.

The requirements to generate interest are within everyone's reach, and some may undoubtedly use these skills to create an appearance of attention and generosity and thus capture their victims, that is, to use a deceptive version of these pillars to start relationships that end in a game of manipulation. On the other hand, it is quite simple to perceive what distinguishes a truly interesting person from a manipulator: character.

Everyone can pay attention, and at this point, it may be difficult to differentiate between genuine and pure attention and attention given with manipulative interests. But the second pillar directly touches on the dimension of character: generosity. The bad character will hardly know how to fake virtue because their personal interest, their extreme selfishness, will always clash with true generosity. Let those who have eyes see. If we observe those who try to be interesting from the perspective of their generosity, we will discover, perhaps without much difficulty, who is nothing but a mere manipulator.

If someone is not making it clear where they want to take you in a relationship, this strongly indicates that there is a hidden personal interest behind their apparent generosity. The devil always shows his tail. We should never use our influence over people in a negative and manipulative way. It is even a factor in destroying relationships.

The interesting person is capable of challenging the other to reach a place they have never reached, to have ideas they never imagined having, to open the consciousness of others to places and things never before seen. Because they want the other's well-being, not their own. There is a desire to make the other greater, to lead them to nobler and more meaningful things.

Whoever is truly interesting desires to open perspectives to free you from a mediocre and massifying view of life. It is a striking trait of the truly interesting person to stand out from mediocrity.

This type of person stands out and is authentic in their own way, positively uplifting everyone around them.

These contrasts make it clear the significant difference between someone who positively influences others and someone who merely aims to be a manipulator. There are coaches and specialists solely focused on small tricks to bend others' wills to act in our interests. It is this type of "relationship technique" that manipulators thrive on. Lasting relationships are not built on this path because the entire foundation of interactions is often the selfish desire to assert one's will.

Our intention in addressing the topic is precisely the opposite. It is to be interesting and authentic using the three pillars to construct a mature personality, making ourselves capable of deeply and enduringly relating to another person, until we achieve the ideal of selfless love. The secret to winning over a loved one in three days is of no use. However, it is truly useful to know how to make the loved one stay for a long time, a time so long it can last until eternity.

Build your inner baggage

As we have deduced from the characteristics associated with the three pillars and also from the distinction between the manipulator and someone with good character,

> **an interesting person is defined by a fundamental trait: they are someone capable of expanding others' psychological consciousness**

— that is, someone who stimulates, through a challenge, the expansion of everything within the repertoire of the individual they relate to.

Contact with a truly interesting person always includes a mixture of positive and challenging feelings, opening our human perspectives. It's someone with whom we exchange a glance, and from there things don't remain the same. In the presence of someone like this, you feel both stronger and weaker, excited and fearful, not quite sure what's happening, discovering with each interaction the kind of person you aim to be. It's, so to speak, touching the untouchable, possessing through an expansive contagion some of the strength and consistency of a unique personality, which appears to you in the form of contact with the unknown and opens new worlds for you.

The interesting person challenges us to break through the shell of our undifferentiated and banal "normality," to launch ourselves toward them in a movement that simultaneously demands a positive transformation of our interior. Being, in some way, challenging to the mental frameworks of others is a trait of someone who is interesting.

At this point, we need to be careful not to rush to produce all these dispositions, in the eagerness to be immediately "interesting." As I have always emphasized, it is a gradual process of inner transformation. I can imagine that for many single people, it may be difficult to contain the anxiety of having someone's attention, of being interesting right away. The lack can generate a kind of desperation that throws us into an emotional free-for-all. "If I'm alone, anyone's attention is worth it, it's better than being alone, after all, all that matters is being loved by someone."

Don't fool yourself. That's not what matters. Not just anyone will do for you. There's a way to build a repertoire, a knowledge baggage in your own way, a way for you to become an authentic person. Many people are unable to answer a simple question: "What do you like?" How can we apply our attention to objects to enrich our repertoire if we can't even answer this elementary question? People who find themselves embarrassed around this question will realize that they don't know how to answer it simply because they've never dedicated time to think about it — a seemingly simple matter that often escapes us in the speed of life's events, in our lack of attention, in the lack of inner retreat and reflection on what's happening with us, on what we experience, and on what we appreciate. For those who have lived life in a semi-automatic mode, the question "What do I like?" can be a mystery or a bitter realization: "Maybe I only like superficial and crude things, things that would never truly make me interesting, or maybe I don't know what I like because nothing I've paid attention to is worthy of appreciation, they're just frivolities."

This is the decisive moment when we awaken to our own presence in the world, to the confrontation with who we are. If until now you couldn't dedicate yourself to a subject for more than two minutes, it's time to give yourself the chance to reflect on which path you want to choose. You don't have a personality because you've never been interested in anything. Start getting interested in various subjects, open yourself to possibilities, and paths will present themselves to your consciousness. Soon you'll be free to choose and recognize what you want and appreciate.

The most intolerant people are the most uninteresting because they close themselves off to things. They say, for example, "I hate left-wing supporters!" "I loathe country music!" and that's it, without extracting any possible benefit from the contact they've had with these realities. It's not necessary to love country music or admire left-wing politics as a way of expanding consciousness, but they're undoubtedly phenomena that exist and influence millions of people.

Opening up to things is recognizing that there are reasons why they exist, and investigating these reasons expands our inner baggage.

The interesting person recognizes the phenomena before them and questions them without intolerance. By doing so, they can discern (because they first wanted to understand) what is just from what is unjust and differentiate between good and evil; in short, this person can exercise judgment on things and authentically knows what *they like and what they don't like.*

Each person has a particular inclination, has their personal affinities. To discover them, you need to be open to things, employing your attention to what presents itself, so that you understand what truly attracts you, what really interests you. It is through the recognition of these personal affinities that bonds will be naturally built. This will allow connections between people to make sense and have the capacity to unfold into long-term relationships. Seeking someone's attention out of mere neediness, being interested in anything the other is interested in, is a relationship without authentic connection that will lead to disappointments.

Maintaining ties with those with whom we have no inner connections, due to the lack of discernment of our inclinations and tastes, produces relationships of dependency. But a lasting and healthy relationship implies an exchange of positive influence, a mutual reinforcement of perceptions, an environment in which both feel comfortable and can produce a fruitful personal exchange. There is no soulmate, only many soulmates. They are those people who can connect with you through a communion of likes, values, and perceptions.

Be interested in what is human

We have already delved into some mechanisms that we need to stimulate in our souls and that will be useful in building an authentic personality. These are principles that will govern our interior, on which we must frequently reflect to achieve the goal of being lucid and attractive people. Now, let's extract from these concepts a practical and direct attitude common to all interesting people.

You need to be open to *human issues*. This is the source of interchangeable subjects among human beings, beyond any specialty. There are people extremely knowledgeable in some particular field who cannot use it to generate genuine human interest. If, for example, civil servants with extensive knowledge of the law, engineers, labor lawyers, marketers, programmers, etc. only have baggage in their own area, if they only know how to talk about very particular knowledge, they will immensely limit the universe of people who will be interested in them, and they will be unpleasant for those who have no contact with their sciences.

Extensive knowledge in technical issues reaches only a restricted audience, which generally is interested in these issues due to some purpose, and not for the subject itself. In human interactions, this specialist will be interesting to very few people, and even

a relationship cannot be based solely on a common specialized interest, because one interest alone does not sustain a lasting bond.

But human subjects are interesting to everyone, allowing for full communication. I will list some examples: topics such as psychology and philosophy, which have existential reach concerning all human beings; politics, which involves common issues to all society — it is from politics that topics with which everyone can connect arise, because everyone's life is to some degree conditioned by political decisions —; history, which is the narrative that connects in a sense all civilizations, ways of life, their wars and dramas (it is no coincidence that in school the history teacher is always the most interesting of the teachers); cinema, literature, and arts in general.

The arts (cinema, literature, painting, and all their manifestations) are capable of presenting various human types, as they make us come into contact with stories that we would never imagine, if not artistically represented. It is through the arts that we become aware of extremely rich characters, who shed light on the deepest depths of human nature. All these subjects are of general interest and will always produce interchangeable interactions.

Occupying your time with these subjects, devoting your attention to these themes will be greatly beneficial for the expansion of your inner repertoire. Delving into these issues will allow for a much richer interaction with others. The same can be said of the topic of religion. Here, creed does not matter, or even the lack of creed. Religion is a dimension universally present in human society. An atheist does not need to believe, but to be interesting, they need to be interested in religion, which is not just submission to God and rites, but a system of human conduct, a repository of philosophy and unique views on the human being. Not to mention the whole set of spiritual knowledge, metaphysical perspectives, miracles, stories, and wonders. No one can say that religion is not something interesting.

Dedicate time to literature, make the effort to read good books, and if you are not inclined to reading, turn to cinema. You don't need to be a *cult* cinephile. Look for lists of the best films ever produced, the list of Oscar winners. If your inclination is visual, dedicate yourself to the appreciation of photography, sculpture, painting. Notice the nuances of the images, feed your inner world with the aesthetic subtlety of forms that always convey meaningful messages to the human being.

It is very pleasant to delight in the physical beauty of a person, with their smell, their haircut, their good taste in dressing. But as our grandmothers wisely said, "that doesn't fill the belly." That will not give concreteness to your relationship. Do not disregard beauty, but be interested above all in the construction of a rich inner world full of truth.

Commit to forming a repertoire within yourself, so that it can be expressed in the world through interaction with your friends, with your partner, with your spouse. It is possible from now on to build new bonds through deeper subjects, grounded in conscious affinities and human themes of universal interest.

There is an authentic personality within you.

It just needs to be found and built.

The problem of language

Let's now investigate some negative forms of human interaction. As we said above, a central resource for the successful performance of interchangeable communications is the construction of a baggage of universally valid human knowledge. But there is a basic assumption, which is the instrument behind all possible interactions: language, which is personal expression and the foundation of communication.

Language problems can be the cause of most difficulties in a relationship, and this applies to singles looking for someone else as well as to married or people in a long-lasting and intimate relationship.

We need to understand that language itself already encloses an ontological problem. This is because human language is a special tool of expression, which sets us apart from other animals. It encompasses nuances and subtleties that are mastered, if we speak of someone well-educated, by conscious intentionality. Through language, a direct and particular experience is transformed into the schematic and communicative expression of what has been lived or experienced.

We use communication to convey lived experiences, something that is within us. It is the expression of our inner life, and through it, we lean towards others, creating connections with our fellow human beings. Just understanding this underscores the importance of language for human relationships. Now, the problem with communication is that most people do not have extensive linguistic tools and cultural symbols necessary for an effective mastery of language.

We are not great literary geniuses, great screenwriters. Generally, people do not have the ability to convey, clearly and richly, their thoughts, which can hinder the creation of meaningful communication bonds with others. And that's natural. There is always a loss in the passage of linguistic expression. Even the greatest writers need to confront this indefinable something in reality, and retreat to the margins of the border of this untranslatable world for common experience.

There will always, therefore, be a noise between what we live and experience and what we can fully communicate to our neighbor. From this, it follows that in many situations we intend to say one thing, but effectively say another. This problem, to some extent, must be faced.

Clearly, we must confront the noise of communication with the utmost effort. Much of this noise can be reduced, and our language can evolve immensely in interpersonal relationships. The goal of our language, if we dedicate ourselves to becoming interesting people, is to approach an authenticity that makes our voice as real as possible to the other, so that we are able to express the maximum of what we would like to convey.

This is the importance of language, and we should be surprised to conclude how underestimated this problem is and how much the majority of people do not worry about improving their linguistic ability at any moment. They prefer to speak using jargon, slang, preconceived ideas, and mental models or diffuse symbols that impregnate the minds of the inattentive through a silent contagion.

Without questioning, without reflecting on the greater or lesser efficiency of their own language, they reproduce ways of speaking from their immediate social circle, childhood cartoons, books they've read, teachers or classmates they've had; ways of thinking from movies, TV, entertainers, social media personalities; they even imitate the mannerisms and quirks of those influences that dominate the universe they "consume".

Note that the problem is not being influenced—those are natural and part of our normal interaction with the world—but allowing oneself to be impregnated by forces in a totally unconscious way, being carried away by the wave, without the concern of expanding and qualifying this same repertoire of influences consciously, in order to incorporate richer traits into one's own language.

In the past, when there was no ease of audiovisual series, it was always common to all educated people the habit of reading, especially poetry. But why read poetry? Note well that poetry often expresses invisible realities, forms of feelings, sensations, details of how something behaves, hints that a scene can evoke, etc. These are not mysteries restricted only to the poet who wrote them and revealed them to the world, but everyday realities experienced by everyone. However, few are capable of expressing them through language, which is why we need poets. The language capable of expressing such subtleties needs to reach a very high level of communicability.

The attentive reading of these great moments of language expression has immense enriching power

for when we have to rely on our own words to clearly express some more subtle or invisible reality that is at the level of our emotions.

The Noises in Romantic Relationships

Here lies the drama of language: not only the inherent difficulty of the word in being faithful to what we want to say, but also the need for the goodwill of the other to listen to us with interest and direct attention to what we say. The accumulated noises of human interaction will remain throughout our lives, and it's easy to see how this can degenerate into complete chaos in relationships.

Now imagine this reality within romantic relationships. For all these reasons of language, affinity, and inherent connection to human interaction, we must be content, yes, to some extent, with a level of friction and noise in prolonged interactions, but we must also take special care with language in a lasting relationship.

In a romantic relationship, there is over time an accumulation of small noises and friction. We gather all these little scars in our sensitivity, and when a new friction arises, we mix it with other past noises that have nothing to do with the present problem, bringing an immeasurable emotional burden to an objectively small issue.

It's difficult to differentiate, in moments of tension, this conglomerate of sensitivities from the specific topic under discussion. The emotional accumulation of noise in interaction resembles waters contained by a dam, and this dam breaks in times of crisis in an emotional torrent, with disconnected problems, producing a communication chaos that prevents any perspective of resolution.

Boyfriends and fiancés tend to have more goodwill in understanding each other because

**they are disarmed of the arsenal of small noises,
the accumulation of which is the product of
prolonged coexistence over time.**

They are more willing to overlook and give fair proportion to these language frictions, due to the hope and enthusiasm that every beginning produces in the hearts of lovers.

Try to have this "beginning" goodwill. This lighter and more understanding disposition that every relationship experiences in its early stages. This sincere disposition not to expect too much in return for affections, to be satisfied with the little that is everything, namely, the presence of the loved one. The enthusiastic attachment to the joy that arises from the mere companionship, so prominent at the beginning of the relationship, reveals in its purity some rehearsal of that unselfish love, which over time moves from natural instinct to conscious goal.

Try to remain somehow united to those instincts that are at the genesis of love. Understand that every topic is just a topic. Hold onto the subjects in the most objective way and with sincere intention for clarity and authenticity in language. Do not always manifest defensively, throwing something unpleasant in the partner's face that has nothing to do with the topic, as if the troubles, misunderstandings, and frictions depended on the unreal justice of a scale where disparate problems should be weighed at all times and must reach a balance, so that neither side has "reason".

The weight of the history of communication noises in a relationship should not be accumulated. These disparate squabbles should not be rigorously cataloged to make a cold accounting of them. The accumulation of interaction noises will naturally occur over time in the relationship. Trying to equate them all, one by one, is impossible, and even more impossible — I would say maddening — would be to equate them all at once, allowing the emotional space between two individuals to carry too heavy a burden of emotional baggage. This will only result in more friction with each new attempt at communication.

Communication in a relationship is a complex and difficult topic to fully pacify. However, the exercise of total presence, attention, clarity, self-criticism, active and present consciousness will make all the difference. Without these efforts, we simply live reactively, from our feelings, from a shapeless inner sensory mass over which we have no control. Without effort to be active and conscious participants in the relationship, we suffer a form of emotional indigestion that will lead to discomfort and ultimately to vomiting. From discomfort and disappointment, we will gain no knowledge, only suffering.

We are endowed with the capacity for communication to master it. It's difficult to have the skill to deal with the emotional dynamics involved in the proper use of language, but the good news is that we are made to be capable of it. In many, the symptom of failure to master this capacity is the resolution of all conflicts through sex. It is in bed that discomfort is pacified and it seems that everything is resolved. And here we have a new illusion, because if outside the most immediate realm of sex and sensations, that is, in the realm of language, dialogue, and thought, two adults cannot resolve themselves, sex will be nothing more than a sedative, no matter how good the "chemistry" of the couple.

What is not resolved in the realm of the spirit will never be resolved solely in the flesh. No one solves anything in bed. Pleasure in these cases is nothing but a "shut up". After orgasm, life goes on and the same problems will repeat themselves unless the couple makes an effort for heart-to-heart dialogue.

We need to know how to communicate to learn to connect our hearts. We need, above all, the willingness to be interested in the other person and actually learn what the other person wants to say to us. We then need goodwill, patience, ears for the other person, to remove from ourselves that exacerbated affective filter that prevents us from putting ourselves in the other's shoes. It's time to stop the habit of formulating a bold response simultaneously with each sentence from the other. Simply stop and listen, without the concern of formulating any response. Give yourself the chance to listen to the other person, lay down your arms, and seek peace, clarity, and truth.

It is not necessary to repeat cliché mantras like "one must be an eternal lover." But it is of great importance to preserve at all costs that spirit of the beginning, even when time and coexistence produce an accumulation of frictions. Keep alive within you that goodwill of the beginnings. Do not carry the unnecessary weight of small frictions.

Seek People, Not Suitors

We talked in the previous chapter about the importance of preserving "the goodwill of beginnings," and how this benevolent, patient, and charitable disposition, common to every beginning of a romantic relationship, is a prelude to the instinctive pursuit of giving ourselves to those we love, an exercise still in its infancy of what can grow and fully manifest in the practice of selfless love — the ultimate goal of human relationships.

Therefore, it is a good time to address the topic of dating. Speaking about dating does not prevent married individuals from benefiting. A married person may realize, upon studying this chapter, various stages they went through with their spouse and quickly identify the shortcomings, their own faults, and omissions in the history of their relationship. They can thus remedy them in some way in their relationship with their partner by better understanding the romantic dynamics originating from dating.

For singles, who are the main stakeholders in the topic, a warning is needed above all. You may have become interested in reading about this because you are looking for a relationship. But I say: this is a wrong approach. You should not be looking for a relationship because this pursuit means looking for a *status* for yourself.

Those who seek a status for themselves are not interested in a person for who they are but are seeking a functionality that another can offer (being a boyfriend or girlfriend).

People today are looking for two things: either sex or marriage. Both the hedonistic pervert, who only thinks about pleasure and wants nothing but to use people's bodies, and the single woman looking for marriage, who is fixated on her "dream," desperate to get married and obtain the *status* of being married, fall into a distorted posture that inevitably leads them to deal with people in a utilitarian manner.

Just as a pervert only sees in others the perspective of their utility for their own pleasure, the one obsessed with the social *status* that a serious relationship produces will be inclined to see others from the perspective of a "good catch," that is, from the standpoint of their utility. It is a tyrannical gaze directed at others. It's seeing others through the lens of personal interest, not from a broad and humane perspective.

I do not mean to say here that aspiring to the *status* of a relationship is inherently immoral. It is indeed desirable. However, this cannot be the driving force of our interest, so that the desire for the other based on their function suppresses all their human dimensions. There are millions of boyfriends and millions of married people in the world, but these human beings are not reduced to being boyfriends or married. Anyone who does not look at the whole person casts a tyrannical gaze upon the individual, seeing them as mere pieces in a project.

It's a very limited perspective on the part of the wife to see her spouse only as a husband. After all, he is a man with a history, aspirations, a professional role, and his own vocations — which undoubtedly include being a husband, a father, etc. These vocations may not have any utility for the wife, or may not even be immediately understood by those in her circle. If this wife is not interested in everything her husband is, the connection between them will be severely compromised.

People have lost genuine interest in the human person. They are in search of a boyfriend, a fiancé, a happy marriage, or in the lowest cases, someone to enjoy life with — a euphemism for someone with whom they can have inconsequential sex.

It is therefore clear the importance, at the beginning of relationships, of a sincere openness to the other as a whole human being. From there will arise the healthiest interactions. It's the goodwill of beginnings.

This goodwill stems from a *loving contemplation* of the other. This idea is not my original creation. I learned it from Professor Olavo de Carvalho, who described it in a homonymous text. Loving contemplation requires a docility towards the reality of the world, that is, docility towards truth, towards reality as it is. Its application to human interactions results in

wanting to contemplate in the other person all their potentialities, the fullness of what they are: their limitations, qualities, positive possibilities, etc.

Those who practice this loving contemplation towards others come to enjoy seeing what the other is.

A very different posture from the one that intends to project onto the other what it desires. Today we see lists of "qualities of the perfect boyfriend," "characteristics of the perfect husband," reports of non-negotiable values that the other must have to be suitable to interest us in a relationship. However good the intentions may be, they are symptoms of the absence of loving contemplation, that is, of a comprehensive and human look at the other.

Those who cast a, so to speak, self-interested gaze at others will content themselves, at best, with what the other already possesses and is the object of their desire, but will never perceive in the other potential beyond their future capabilities and all the goods that can blossom from that soul. Knowing someone based on these criteria is to engage in great self-deception. People are not born ready. The person you know today is not a crystallized and immutable form. None of us is completely whole; we live in a process of manifesting potentials. Clinging only to what the other already has and pleases us is to take them as a frozen being in time and space, incapable of manifesting new forms.

People Are Mutable

It is necessary, therefore, to love everything about another person, with special and authentic interest in knowing the traits that displease us the most. Acting in this way avoids, from the outset, false expectations, which are nothing more than projections of an enthusiastic mind regarding qualities that do not exist in a person with whom we are beginning to relate. Here is the harsh truth: human beings cannot be fairly judged by a *checklist* of qualities on the first encounter.

Married individuals will understand this reality more easily. Spouses clearly notice, given the continued experience of the relationship over time, that their partner undergoes immense changes. Of course, there is an essence, an existential foundation that remains. But it would not be an exaggeration to say that those who marry will live with several "people" over time, if we improperly take someone's way of existing, thinking, and acting at a given moment in their history as a person. Married people know: individuals are capable of changing significantly over the course of a life story.

Marriage itself is a space of interaction oriented towards this process. It is in marriage that spouses, by helping each other, change, take on new forms, and are marked by experiences, difficulties, and events. Even couples in longer-term relationships experience the first signs of transformation. In a relationship lasting two or three years, that passionate couple from the first week is no longer the same as the one preparing for engagement. It's a fact of life.

Do not understand the loving openness to the mutable character of the other as a blank check to relate to anyone. After all, everyone will be a different person in the future. It's not about that. You need to find someone with important points of connection to avoid excessive energy expenditure. However,

> **even the "right person" will change, will adapt over time, with experience and the multiple movements generated by loving interaction.**

Consider this a natural starting point.

Go to your first date with an open mind. Turn what is foreign into familiar, without a rigid confrontation with the nature of the other person. Have a genuine interest in the other person, a desire to know their authenticity, without clinging to your own expectations of what a "perfect boyfriend" should be, and without turning the fruitful interaction with another human being into a meeting that needs a kind of "efficiency." Remove from your mind the thought that you cannot "waste time on a date" if it's not to find a good boyfriend.

There is no wasted time when we are opening ourselves to the perspective of others. At worst, you will have met another human soul, with part of their history, dreams, desires, inclinations, which already enriches your inner baggage. Dismiss your own desires when approaching the other person. Open yourself to a new human being with a sincere disposition and, cheerfully, cast a contemplative gaze.

Be more interested in your own capacity to lovingly contemplate the other person. It will be much easier to forgive flaws and, more importantly, to get to know the other person. By doing so, you will gain a more secure knowledge to determine if a deeper connection is possible.

Be kind to other people. Don't think of the other as a potential suitor. Just think of them as José, João, Maria. Connections for deeper bonds occur betwhen people, not between you and this abstract and cruel portrayal of a "suitor." Even initial differences of opinion, such as in political or ideological matters, are not definitive marks of separation in early contacts. You don't have to completely shut yourself off from the other when some noise arises. Not all opinions stated are seriously held or deeply considered, and not all disagreements are serious obstacles to other possible convergences, which are much more decisive for the connection between two people.

Remove anxiety from your mind, the desperation to be committed right away, and — especially for women — the desperation to get married, to avoid being left on the shelf. Think that rushing through this process recklessly could land you in an unhappy marriage, and being in that condition can be such a source of multiple problems for your life that following a sensible pace will never be cause for regret.

Marrying hastily with someone who merely meets, by some twist of fate, part of the requirements of your "perfect man" checklist is no guarantee of a healthy and happy marriage.

Anyone considering marriage should bear in mind that this is one of those supreme life decisions. Haste does not compensate for the risk of getting into trouble.

On the other hand, maintaining one's own sensible pace within a relationship will result in a much more genuine and kind posture. It is a process that, although it may have variable timing, compensates for the richness of having the opportunity to incline oneself to another heart, to seek it as one seeks patiently the gestures of true communion. To achieve this, it is not necessary for the first date to end with a kiss. Lightness is needed. It is not necessary to sabotage yourself by insisting on an interaction where there are clearly repugnant traits for you. But it is also not about closing oneself rigidly without making an effort to have a light posture with another, then unknown. When the other person realizes that we are open, they also tend to open up to us, and this gives us more freedom to be who we are.

There is a considerable example of this genuine interest that I advocate in couples from 40 or 50 years ago. I don't mean to say that in our parents' time there were no selfish and frivolous interests or people who were looking for chaos in the wake of sexual liberation. But, generally speaking, there was a more sincere interest in the other person, in getting to know people for who they were and not based on some expectation of a social role.

There was a greater connection between hearts in the past, so people leaned towards each other for who they were and not for projections cast upon the other. It seems to me that relationships in that period were lighter. Try an experiment and ask your parents how they met. The impression their story should generate is that those human encounters were more genuine – and I'm not talking here about moral purity, complete correctness of actions according to religious criteria, etc. I'm talking about authenticity and lightness in interactions.

Dating is meant to end

There wasn't so much drama in the past about the topic of "dating." Dating is a period that should be for discernment. It's two partners gathering elements for a decision valid for a lifetime. The end is to solidify a commitment to be faithful to each other and loyal to this common project. Today, dating is overrated; it's almost an end in itself. Instead of being seen as a transitional period with an end date, it is held with much more attachment, as a kind of marriage without the serious commitments of marriage, which gives a very sentimental character to this experience, which is nothing more than a commitment with lasting aspirations without the depth of a permanent promise.

In this process of sanctification of dating, people stay together for years, some couples even reach a decade together, but there is never any mention of the definitive commitment of marriage. At most, there is a pragmatic test drive when the decision for the couple to live together arises. And after a long time invested and a lot of emotional energy expended, the end becomes the most terrifying of prospects.

Things shouldn't work this way. Every breakup is fair because every dating relationship needs an expiration date. Every dating relationship is a period that serves for discernment between two parties. The natural end of a lasting relationship is the total commitment of both to a common project sealed by a sacred oath. That's what the institution of marriage is for. No one would have any problem breaking up if the value attributed to dating were not so exaggerated.

Therefore, do not unnecessarily prolong a dating relationship that will lead nowhere; do not take a breakup so seriously. Do not beg the other person to marry you. Both need to have the same desire. What benefit is there in persuading someone who does not want marriage to marry you for life? If your interest is marriage and the other's is not, the conclusion is very simple, although difficult to accept: time to say goodbye. Let each one go their own way.

Dating is not the final commitment,

it was made so that we have a chance to go back — or to move forward, breaking up to make room for marriage.

Have the intention to see the other and to be good. Do not seek in the other only the fulfillment of a role. It is in the source of authentic love that the deepest and most lasting bonds can arise that will be consistent with the promises of marriage. We start from the loving contemplation of the other and the good spirit towards the other to gradually reach the selfless love that one is only capable of directing towards a spouse — and the spouse is the partner we will defend and be permanent companions to. The fruits of conjugal love form a family.

The Seasons of Romantic Relationships

To better explain the phases that a romantic relationship typically goes through, I'll use the metaphor of *seasons*. I'll use the image of the seasons as analogies for the periods couples go through, point out some conclusions, and summarize the natural movements in a relationship.

The seasons of the year are phenomena that cause cyclical changes in the world. Spring, summer, autumn, and winter: there is a symbolic correlation between these seasons and the elements air, fire, earth, and water, respectively. Spring correlates with air because it's light, moist, and warm. Summer correlates with fire, which is warm and dry. Autumn is cooler, but there's still a dryness that causes leaves to fall; it correlates with earth, with dryness, and with cold. Winter is cold and wet and is related to water, which also holds these characteristics.

Let's see what can be drawn from the correlation between these elements and the seasons with relationships. After all,

human relationships can also correspond to cyclical patterns.

While there are many differences between relationships taken by themselves, we can perceive that there are formal similarities among all of them, which are even evident to common sense. Let's see what this consists of.

Spring

What would we say is the spring of relationships? Spring is related to air. It's warm and moist. Warmth brings expansion. Boiling water expands and evaporates, ascending outward. Everything warm grows. And what is moist? It's that which envelops us. Water in a container contours and fills its entire shape. It adapts, has fluidity, a dynamism that implies enveloping expansion. It's the trait of moisture.

What is, after all, the spring of relationships? It's that moment when you've just met the person, creating the first bonds, letting yourself be enveloped by them and enveloping them in turn. There's a natural expansion because you want to be part of the other.

The couple constantly wants to talk, wants to be together.

This warm need for identification and involvement is characteristic of beginnings and also of spring. Everything is pleasant, everything is fluid and good. All beginnings are always enjoyable.

Summer

But after spring comes summer. The humidity and freshness of spring are modified by the heat of summer, which dries. In the relationship's summer, there is still expansion, still an impulse toward the other, but dryness begins. Edges begin to sharpen, the first friction emerges. Unpleasant traits in the other start to be noticed. After the first joyful and enthusiastic season where everything about the other was pleasant, a deepening of the relationship reveals the less engaging traits that were ignored or even hidden.

It's the stage in dating when a combative trait emerges. It's realized that not everything is fantasy and poetry.

The phase where everything was light has passed.

There's still an inner fire that binds the couple, but the phase of friction begins. The relationship becomes less light and more difficult, and not everything is enjoyable. The couple begins to understand that they are two different people, with different projects, with distinct natures. This is the time for important conversations about fundamental values. It's the time for the conflicting agreement between the parties at a point in the relationship where there is full openness of the self.

Fully opening up and, so to speak, "revealing everything" about ourselves is an important passage in every relationship. Someone might think they wouldn't want to go through the summer of relationships because they hate friction, but stages in these seasons of romantic relationships cannot be skipped. What we should do is face them as necessary steps in ascending to a more mature and complete union with the other.

All these phases need to be experienced. Don't try to skip them. There's no good or bad phase, but only stages that are part of the natural cycle of romantic interaction between human beings. Every relationship needs to deal with and absorb the lessons of each stage. Every couple sincerely seeking to unite needs to desire to live through these stages in the most active and fruitful way.

Autumn

After summer comes autumn, which represents the crucible for relationships. Autumn is the presence of earth. The heat of summer begins to cool and hands over its dryness to autumn. It's the period of cold and dryness. This signifies for relationships a critical moment. Edges become sharper than ever, the rigidity of clashes in the relationship takes on a more violent and definitive character. These clashes are no longer compensated for by the still-living warmth in the relationship in its summer phase, which often masks the moral reach of some differences between the couple. Here conflicts manifest coldly.

Cold has the property of contracting things, unlike warmth, which expands them. In autumn, after the couple has defined their boundaries—what is pleasant for one and the other, as this concerns essential differences in ways of existence—it's time to gather all the information about what each one is, with the acceptance of all vectors of conflict and convergence, and settle into a state of rest.

From now on, little will be new, and that enthusiasm of the beginnings, called by some "passion," will fade. Until then, the relationship had a taste of poetry and adventure.

Entering this season suppresses the romantic atmosphere and begins a new, more calculated, more rational phase in the couple's interaction.

It's a period of careful analysis of the relationship, a time for the most serious reflections on the connection built between the two, the main affinities and ruptures, in order to reach cold and rational conclusions about the future of the relationship.

This is the opportune moment for important decisions. It's the time when we will have more baggage to decide whether it's worth continuing the relationship or not. Will it be the relationship's autumn, the time for leaves to fall and the end of dating, or the time to carry on with the promise until winter? It's the time to definitively address pending issues to move forward or to keep everything as it is and break up.

Winter

Those who accept the promise reach winter. Water is damp and cold. The dryness begins to disappear with the moisture, but the cold remains. That springtime union returns, and one partner envelops the other under a new key. The unity of the couple is greatly strengthened, the homogeneity between the parties, which become more malleable and docile, reaches its peak. It's no longer the warm and, so to speak, free involvement of springtime.

The winter of relationships is a stable and decisive union. Calm and tolerant.

It's the couple entering the maturity of the relationship.

Solid, concise, united, in communion forever.

Forgiveness

It's time to say the final words on relationships. We've reflected on total loving surrender for unselfish love, practiced virtues to truly be interesting, and learned to find authentic connections with others. We've also reflected on the loving bonds that arise from genuine interest in another person, through loving contemplation, and we've gone through all the seasons of relationships. Now, there's one final lesson, the most important to sustain a lasting interaction.

Everything we've discussed so far about romantic relationships culminates in this final theme: forgiveness. Immediately, the topic may suggest adultery to many. It must be said, first and foremost, that adultery cannot be dissociated from forgiveness. But something deeper must be examined in this issue: why is adultery the first thing that comes to mind when forgiveness in a relationship is mentioned?

Why are we obsessed with adultery?

Adultery signifies the other's infidelity towards us. However, is that the only thing that can be considered the most unforgivable act of all? Let's consider the wide range of neglect, humiliation, defamation, offenses, and omissions we inflict on each other over years of relationship. The inescapable conclusion is that we are all flawed and miserable. We offend each other and break our promises every day. So why does adultery come to mind first when we think of forgiveness? Is it truly the worst offense in a relationship? Some even say, "I forgive everything except infidelity." Isn't this conviction of adultery as an "unforgivable sin" the result of other forces at play in the moral imagination of our time?

Aren't we too involved in our own ego and hypersensitive to anything that socially stains us?

The serious commitment of marriage is made before God. Those who betray are not just betraying the other, but above all betraying God. But in our time, it's we who believe ourselves deserving of exclusive fidelity pledged, first and foremost, to God.

"I've made many mistakes, but I've never even looked at anyone else. That's why I can't forgive infidelity." Whoever can say this should thank God for having this virtue, but shouldn't consider themselves perfect because of it. You may be perfect in this regard, but terribly flawed in many others, not only with your spouse, but with your neighbor as well. If God, even being perfect and deserving of all respect, forgives many sins, do we, so flawed, have the right to demand impeccable justice when we are offended? It's always pride that's behind the feeling that an offense is unforgivable.

We marry flesh-and-blood people. People full of flaws, wounded by original sin, just like us. We're not dealing with gods and saints, but with fallen individuals seeking mercy. Creating an unreal concept in the mind that no one can reveal their miseries is, ultimately, a cruelty to others. We don't have the definitive right to condemn someone for an unforgivable sin. The only sin we know to have this condition is the one that offends the Holy Spirit. How foolish must we be to believe that any offense against us cannot be forgiven? If this hasn't been enough to convince that adultery isn't the most serious of crimes, let's reflect on an example. There's a Jewish story that tells of a compulsive and repentant slanderer meeting his rabbi. "What should I do to fix everything I've done?" says the slanderer. The rabbi replies: "Go up to the top of a tower and tear open a feather pillow. Then come back here." The sinner did as he was asked. He tore the pillow from the top of the tower, and the feathers floated everywhere with the wind. The penitent returned to the rabbi, who said to him: "Now, go back to the city and retrieve every feather that scattered."

This is what slander consists of. What seemed like a small act — speaking ill of someone to another — spreads from mouth to mouth, from whisper to whisper, until it reaches gigantic proportions for the reputation of the slandered. Slander is an act that few people refrain from and has some degree of irreparable harm. Tracing every consequence of the sin of slander is an impossible task. It's an injustice that cannot be completely repaired, even for the repentant. Adultery, on the other hand, is a crime against one person and repairing it is a much simpler task. I ask: why does everyone say that in a relationship adultery is the only unforgivable crime, if speaking ill of one's spouse to others, that is, slandering them, is considered trivial? We often reflect little on the evil deeds we commit. Adultery is obviously not normal or light. No one gets married expecting to be betrayed. After all, marriage implies an oath of fidelity. But have we asked forgiveness for other evils, which can be as bad or worse than adultery in some contexts? Do we really have the moral sensitivity to perceive, as in the example above, that speaking ill of one's spouse to others is an act of serious infidelity? In the particular case of adultery, there's immense cultural focus on the subject. Novels, soap operas, and movies incessantly depict adultery. The theme is so hammered into our minds that it has become a kind of obsession: as if in a romantic relationship there were no other crimes,

**as if everything else were just a minor slip, because
the only evil that exists is called adultery.**

Now, let's remember the story of the repentant slanderer. He cannot repair the harm he caused. But how could a penitent adulterer repair his wrong? If he repented, he can ask forgiveness from the one he betrayed, definitively cut ties with the lover, become a much better person, never fall back into betrayal, etc. What's the irreparable damage in this situation? The loss of trust? We can say yes, but it's an abstract damage, something in the inner world. It's not a concrete, effective damage, implying constant harm, as in the case of slander.

Trust is nothing more than a fetish. Proof of this is that no matter how much trust you place in someone, it can always be betrayed. Clinging to the feeling of trust as if it were the most important force to unite two people in love is futile. Trust is based on real data, on the experience of the solidity of the other's actions. But this doesn't guarantee that the other will never hurt you. Remember: we're dealing with humans, not gods.

"Having trust" is very dear to all of us because we have a huge attachment to security. We absolutely refuse to live in a world of insecurity where anything can happen at any moment. However, it's necessary to recognize that all the feeling of trust in the world doesn't guarantee us anything concrete in reality. It's this perception that allows us to receive offenses in a proportionate manner, without exaggerating them because they offended our fetishes, but weighing them by their actual weight.

Never bet on your desire for security. Bet on your strength, because it's what will concretely move you in difficult times if something disrupts your world, if you confront some vile act, or if you're a victim of injustice. It's your strength in dealing with a problem that will help you overcome it. The feeling of security will be of no use.

There's a Hierarchy of Evil

Don't take another step in this subject trying to minimize the seriousness of adultery. We need to separate fetishes and obsessions of an era from the actual weight of offenses. Adultery is always wrong. It's always condemned in sacred codes wherever there's a healthy human civilization. But not forgiving violates a greater commandment.

Why close yourself off to the possibility of forgiveness when this attitude is greater than any sin?

There's a hierarchy of sins and human evils. People have come to give disproportionate importance to lust, as if it were the source of the worst sins in a relationship, when in fact the worst of all is pride. Feeling so above the offender that you exercise the right not to forgive them is typical of pride. We must admit: being proud is a much greater evil than being an adulterer.

I want to propose a meditation on the gravity of the harm we cause to others. Think about all the offenses you've committed against someone, all the small omissions over the years of the relationship, all the little manipulations, all the half-truths and self-serving lies, the hidden offenses and blackmail, pretending to be tired just to avoid helping someone in need, creating deceptive difficulties when it wasn't in your own interest to give, the times you didn't bring joy, or weren't there for the other when they needed you most.

You must create within yourself the awareness that you too are flawed and evil. You must also understand that the other is not a demigod. From there arises the possibility of looking at the evil in the other without cruel scrutiny. This is a defense mechanism because we're terrified of being hurt.

Forgiveness is the foundation of human coexistence. Why do we close ourselves off to the possibility of forgiving precisely the person we love the most and to whom we have given ourselves the most? Wouldn't this person be the most deserving of such a gesture? Let us know that the tacit promise of every marriage can be described in a few words that may harden our hearts if we let self-interest dominate us: "I promise to forgive you forever. I will be your eternal advocate, never your judge. I will stand by your side even in the face of your worst sins."

People prefer to live relationships based on fear, eager to find fault in the other to drink from the wound of love for the feeling of superiority. Most marriages today are sustained by fear. There's no foundation in inner fidelity, the one that knows how to forgive those we love, a forgiveness that carries the longing not to wish condemnation upon your beloved.

Because the desire of lovers is to remain united forever. And to be able to be together in this place beyond time, they will need to go through the judgment of the one who said: "forgive us our trespasses as we forgive those who trespass against us." The lover who knows the miseries of the beloved does not desire their condemnation, but wants their forgiveness, and by desiring it, begins to forgive them themselves. Love does not want justice; it grants mercy.

Some people are very afraid of social consequences, of being recognized as "cuckolds" for the rest of their lives. But consider how many betrayals occur among human beings every day. How many of these people are recognized for a lifetime just for being betrayed? Secondly, why should we ourselves be so indiscreet as to, instead of keeping such pain within the intimacy of a wounded couple, publish to the world the miseries of those who betray us in order to seek revenge, as if hurting oneself were somehow revenge? All of this involves many ego problems. In a time of betrayal, it is always possible to stop and reflect retrospectively on the causes that generated the problem.

Betrayal never happens overnight.

The wonderful husband who never gave any reason to doubt doesn't cheat without a story that led to his downfall. Everyone knows that betrayal doesn't work that way. The cause is not necessarily the fault of the betrayed, but it always exists and can be described.

Those who can be very honest with themselves will be able to understand their contribution to the other's wickedness. Often it's quite possible to know where the problem lies and how to solve it. However, the blame for the betrayal always lies with the one who betrays. The act of betrayal is always a free decision. The traitor can never use these supposed causes that "led" them to betray to justify their unjust act. Those who betray and receive the grace of forgiveness, moreover, need to prove many things to their partner from then on. It's something that causes many scars.

The true posture of one who repents is an act of contrition. Those who are truly repentant ask forgiveness from the one they offended like a beggar asking for alms on the street. If the one who betrays is truly repentant, they want, even in this sad hour, the well-being of their spouse. That's why they'll have this humble posture to facilitate the difficult movement of forgiveness in their partner as much as possible.

The act of contrition comes along with all the weight of the flaws of the one who betrays. It's an act that needs to carry all the weight of freedom, the same freedom that led someone to betray. The act of contrition is a plea for mercy. In the end, it's the mortified admission that your life is in the hands of the one you offended. The attitude towards the betrayed must be one of total humility and mortification. On the other hand, it's not good for the one who broke fidelity and repented to fall into a process of self-flagellation.

The penance of the traitor who did wrong is now to do good. Nothing can be more difficult — and in a way edifying — than to humble oneself and acknowledge an error in all its depth. The victims of betrayal are God and the partner, and to both we must direct an honest plea for forgiveness. But

> **if someone falls into a cycle of self-destruction out of remorse, they will lack the moral strength to commit a dignified act, which is to try to repair a great harm.**

If you are a traitor, don't accuse yourself to the point of self-destruction. You'll need to be whole to rise and patiently prove, for a long time, the value of your true repentance.

A meditation on forgiveness

Whenever we feel hurt and wounded by those we love, it seems to us that the pain of these offenses is greater. Even knowing our own faults and how they don't entitle us to feel untouchable, the person we love the most is the last one from whom we expect a wound. It's a natural dynamic of our minds. The experience of this pain is recorded by the psalmist: "Even my best friend, in whom I trusted, who shared my bread, has betrayed me!"

Many come to understand that the other is human and capable of offending us. But it's certain that no one gets married expecting to be betrayed and offended, even though it's always a very real possibility. Needless to say, those who marry and don't even imagine this possibility will be intensely frustrated. We conceive of an ideal world, and dealing with life as it is isn't easy.

That's why you should always practice a reality check, thinking to yourself: "I can be hurt in this life, but I need to bet on my strength, on my love for others, and on how that love is capable of making me continue to love, even giving up on rightful revenge, never allowing an offense to destroy what is good in me, nor extinguish my enthusiastic hope in the best of those I love."

There's an inner mechanism that manifests in three stages when we're offended. First, there's a bitter taste. Even when willing to forgive, this bitterness will be present, and this noble gesture won't reward us with immediate relief. A desire arises in us for the offender to also suffer the consequences of the pain that has struck us.

But then, secondly, comes the conviction that there's a value greater than the pain. Deep down, we know that we're not endowed with justice or the ability to judge. Those who forgive hand over justice to those who have the power and capacity to judge. From this comes a relief, which is the relief of not having to be a judge.

Finally, the possibility of forgiveness arises. Every truly good person, who is trying to walk the path of perfection, who is trying to be better, and especially one who seeks all this because they are Christian, in situations where anger and revenge try to crush their heart, will find an appeal within themselves for forgiveness. We desire to forgive, especially our loved ones. Deep down, we know this to be the noblest stance. Forgiveness is what we would like to achieve.

This person who feels the desire to forgive is capable of realizing that their beloved offender also suffers for having offended them.

The person desires to forgive because they long to alleviate the suffering of the repentant loved one.

It's a mistake to think that hatred is the opposite of love. The offended would no longer love the one who offended them if betrayal didn't cause pain. Because it's in indifference that the absence of love lies. If it hurts and generates hatred, it's because we're outraged by those we love. However deeply an offense from a loved one may strike us, however much it stirs great hatreds within us, let's not deceive ourselves by quickly saying that love has ended.

Another mistake of those who intend to forgive is trying to forget the offense, as if nothing had happened. It's true that emotionally the soul of the wounded would prefer that such an event had never occurred. How we wish that those we love had not offended us! We set out to seek healing for the wound without facing it head-on. Clinging to distractions, we immerse ourselves in daily tasks and work to forget, turning the offense into a taboo. How many deceived people believe this to be forgiveness! There's something abstract and emotional in the soul. But there's also something very different in its rational dimension. Unless there's a biochemical issue, our rational soul will never forget an offense simply because it happened. Forcing the soul to erase what it cannot only generates more frustration. The event exists and will always be etched in memory.

We love the truth even against our will. It imposes itself on our conscience. What happened, happened. There's no point opposing the truth with the creation of the most convenient fantasies. But it's natural for us to act in this world according to our baggage, our truth, everything that has happened to us. Those who deny what happened, sooner or later, will find themselves invaded again by that same anger when the memory of the offense surprises their memory. And it's not uncommon for them to, at these times, throw their partner's past crimes back in their face, in a futile manner that will only exacerbate the wound.

To remain sane, it's better to accept a fact: to live with bad memories forever. Because the internal movement of true forgiveness implies a choice. Do you want to rid yourself of your pain and all the bad consequences of the offense, or do you want to free both yourself and the repentant offender from this pain? Do you want justice to prevail at all costs, and for the other to suffer to the maximum, or do you wish for your offender to be rewarded for what they did — instead of suffering for what they did? Hence arises another question: can my offender be rewarded? Well, someone who commits an offense and truly repents, receiving forgiveness, always becomes better than they were before. Because before there was an offender who acted freely to hurt their loved one. Now there's a repentant human being who has undergone the humiliation of admitting they were wrong and is following a new course.

Those who grant forgiveness, besides wishing for the suffering to leave their heart through this act, also aim for their offender to fully receive the gift that can be derived from the humiliation of their own repentance, from the awareness of their own misery. That is, to be a new person.

If you desire eternity for your loved one, and intend to walk alongside that person in a permanent union, you cannot wish for your loved one to suffer permanently for their mistakes.

Especially those united by the bond of matrimony need, as if by duty, to extend forgiveness to their spouse for this spiritual reason. A couple cannot walk together towards eternity when one of the parties continues to harbor hatred towards something in the other. Therefore, we must destroy our desire for justice and hand it over to whom it rightfully belongs, which is God Himself.

Thus, a man and a woman can walk together with steady steps, even amidst so many clashes and so much pain, even with misunderstandings, even under the weight of bearing human miseries that are always lurking, whispered by the wind by invisible evil advisors. It's necessary to love others as we love ourselves. If we forgive as we always desire to be forgiven, we need not fear chance or misfortune. It's a completely free act and independent of circumstances. It's finally feeling the ultimate union, goodwill, patience, joy, taste, the selfless surrender of everything: love.

About the Author

Varsha Bhargava is a fresh voice in the literary world, with a background in journalism and a passion for exploring the complexities of the human experience, Varsha brings a unique perspective to her writing.

As an author, Varsha is committed to pushing boundaries and challenging conventions, using her platform to shed light on important social issues and amplify marginalized voices. With each new project, she aims to inspire and provoke thought, inviting readers to question, reflect, and empathize.